EXPLORING THE PAST

EXPLORING FARMING

Ralph Whitlock

Illustrated by Stephen Wheele

Wayland

Exploring the Past

Exploring Buildings
Exploring Clothes
Exploring Communications
Exploring Farming
Exploring Industry
Exploring People
Exploring Schools
Exploring Shopping
Exploring Sport and Recreation
Exploring Transport

Cover: *Hop pickers at work on a Kent farm, 1910.*

Series Editor: Stephen Setford
Designed by: David Armitage

First published in 1987 by
Wayland (Publishers) Ltd
61 Western Road, Hove
East Sussex, England BN3 1JD

British Library Cataloguing in Publication Data
Whitlock, Ralph
Exploring farming. – (Exploring the past).
1. Agriculture – Great Britain – History
– Juvenile literature
I. Title II. Series
630′.941 S455

ISBN 1 85210 004 4

Phototypeset by Kalligraphics Ltd, Redhill, Surrey
Printed by in Italy by G. Canale & C.S.p.A., Turin
Bound by in the U.K. by The Bath Press, Avon

Contents

1 Introduction

We explore the past because we are interested to know what people did and how they lived in the past. However, the past need not be many hundreds of years ago: it can be last year, last week, or even yesterday.

Exploring farming in the past may seem a little difficult if you live in a town, because you may not often get to see a farm. However, you can get some idea of what happens on the farm by observing the changing of the seasons and how they affect the things which grow in your local park. Similarly, the work of a farmer depends largely upon the seasons, as it always has. In spring, the time when new plant life emerges, the farmer sows the seed for the year's crops. In summer the crops grow to maturity, and in autumn, when they are ripe, they are harvested. In winter, the farmer is busy keeping the animals fed and comfortable, and preparing for the next year.

A ewe and her lamb. When you see farm animals, try to think why they are kept by farmers. Sheep, for instance, provide us with meat, milk (in some countries) and wool to make clothes.

Above *The farmer's work still depends largely on the seasons. You may be able to guess what is happening on the farm by watching the changing of the seasons in your local park.*

Left *If your parents have an allotment or garden, you can watch plants and vegetables develop through the year, just as they do on farms.*

Farmers carried out the same basic tasks in the past as they do today. Methods have changed and farmers use different tools, but the seasons which control all their activities are much the same as they have been for several thousand years.

Remember also that most towns and cities are built on what used to be farmland. You may find, from looking at old maps in your local library, that your area had very strong links with farming, even though it is built-up today.

Do you have any grandparents or elderly neighbours whom you could ask questions about the past? If so, what can they tell you about farming when they were young? Perhaps they lived for a time on a farm during the Second World War. Many people, especially children, were evacuated to the countryside and learned to help on farms, doing such things as picking fruit, harvesting potatoes and feeding calves and lambs. Ask them what crops grew on the farm, what animals the farmer kept, and the changes that have occurred in farming during their lifetime.

If you happen to live in the country or at the edge of a town, you will have a good start for the study of this book. If not, the book may encourage you to visit the countryside or spend your holidays there. Perhaps there is a town farm nearby which you can visit? Local libraries and museums will be good starting points for gathering information about local farming.

In the picture below, you can see some of the 600 boys and girls from London schools who helped with the 1942 harvest on farms owned by the London County Council. If you or your parents know any older people who helped on farms during the Second World War, ask them what memories they have of that time.

2 General farming

Look at the birds in your garden or on your school playing-fields. What are they doing? They are almost certainly searching for food. At some times of the year they find plenty; at others it is difficult for them to find enough. All birds and animals have to rely on what food they can find around them, though some have learned to store it.

In the distant past, people faced the same problems. Our earliest ancestors gathered berries and fruits and dug up roots to eat. They were also hunters, pursuing or laying traps for animals, which they ate. They also learned to store food, drying meat and fish for winter use.

Later, in Neolithic times (4000–1800 BC), they discovered how to grow plants, by sowing seed

A red fox rummages through the contents of an overturned dustbin. Wild animals spend much of their time looking for food. In the distant past, people lived like this too, hunting animals and searching for berries and fruits.

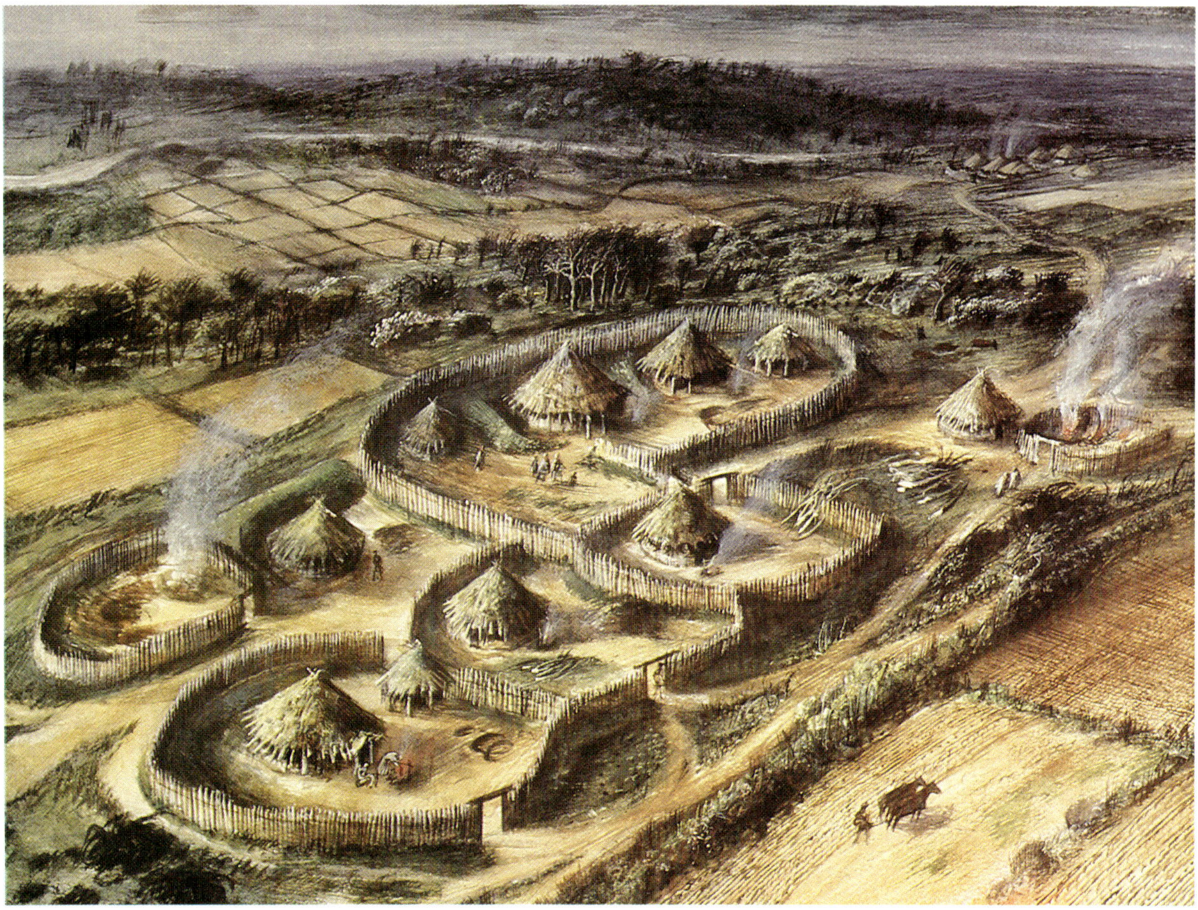

A Bronze Age farming settlement, around 500 BC. At night, the animals were brought into the safety of the fenced enclosures to protect them from wild animals.

and gathering the new seeds when ripe. They learned to domesticate animals, from which they could obtain meat, milk, wool and leather. And so they became farmers. Each family produced enough for its own needs. Farming of this sort is called subsistence farming and is still carried on in many parts of the world. In fact, we all have farmers for ancestors.

When people started to farm they quickly altered the landscape. Once Britain was mostly covered by forests, but people had to cut down the trees and clear the land to make fields for growing their crops. If you had been a child in those days you would have had to spend most of your time keeping the farm animals from straying into the forest or into growing crops. At night the farm animals were brought into a fenced enclosure to protect them from wolves and bears, and someone always had to be on guard.

Farming today

Today, as in the past, farmers grow things and keep domestic animals mostly to provide food. Go to a supermarket and make a list of the different sorts of food there. Concentrate first on basic foods produced in this country, such as butter, milk, cereals, eggs, bread, meat, cheese, jam and so on. Mark against each item the crop or animal from which it is derived.

You will find that some of the items in the supermarket are produced by farmers in other countries. Many of the foods we eat have to come from countries with warmer climates than our own. Make a list of these foods and the countries they come from. See if you can identify the plant or animal responsible for each.

If you visit small farms in the hilly and more remote parts of Britain, such as the Scottish Highlands and the Welsh Mountains, you will find that most of the crops are grown to provide food for animals in winter, when grass is scarce.

On bigger farms in the lowlands, however, most of the crops are grown for human consumption, and you will probably see very big machines at work. Here, farming has been thoroughly mechanized. Because machines are so expensive, many farms have become specialized. There are arable farms, which specialize in growing crops; and dairy farms, which specialize in milk production. Can you think of others? Make your own list. Does it include stock farms, which breed and rear animals, pig farms, sheep farms, poultry farms, fruit farms and vegetable or horticultural farms (also called market gardens)?

Above *Britain imports a lot of food from other countries. When you next visit shops and markets, try to find out where the food you buy comes from.*

Below *Many farms, like the pig farm in this picture, now concentrate on just one type of agriculture.*

3 Hay and silage

Dig a small plot of land and leave it for several weeks. What happens? Lots of weeds come up, because their seeds are already in the soil. If you leave it for several years, grass will probably become the dominant crop. The damp climate of Britain is ideal for growing grass.

Many farm animals (such as sheep, horses, geese, goats and donkeys, but not pigs) live largely on grass. So in some fields the farmer grows grass for these animals to eat.

Because Britain has a long winter when grass and other plants stop growing, the farmer has to store grass for the animals to eat in winter. Supposing you had to store grass for the winter, how would you set about it? The simplest way would be to cut and dry it. Dried grass is called hay. In the past, almost every farmer made hay. If you know an elderly person who has helped on a farm they will almost certainly be familiar with haymaking. Ask them about it, and make notes on how they went about it.

A mediaeval farming scene, showing grass being mown for hay.

Hay-making in the old-fashioned way, at the turn of the century, when most farming tasks were still performed by hand.

Modern farmers often cut the grass in spring while it is still growing fast, and compress it tightly in a large pit, to get rid of the air. Grass preserved in this way is called silage.

Farmers today also grow turnips, kale and other crops to help out with winter supplies of food for domestic animals. However, before the seventeenth century, farmers had no such crops to rely on. So in November they had a slaughter day, when surplus animals were killed and salted down for winter use. In England it was usually associated with St Martin's Day (9 November). Everyone then had a feast of fresh meat.

What other seasonal dishes can you think of? Strawberries in July. Apples in October. Turkeys at Christmas. Ducks in summer, when they can

Left *In spring, many farmers cut the fresh green grass to make silage for the animals to eat later in the year. The farmer uses a machine called a forage harvester, like the one in the picture.*

be eaten with green peas. Nowadays thanks to refrigeration, we can enjoy fresh meat, fruit and vegetables all the year round.

In hill areas, because of the harsh climate, it was even more important to get rid of surplus animals before winter set in. For this reason thousands of cattle were rounded up annually in the Scottish Highlands and driven to the great fairs at Crieff and Falkirk, where many were sold to English buyers. Drovers were often then hired to drive the animals as far south as Essex, where they were fattened on rich pastures for the London market. The drovers followed regular routes known as droveways, skirting the smaller towns to avoid paying tolls. Now that those towns have grown you will often find a Droveway or Drove Road not far from the centre.

Find Crieff, Falkirk, Essex and London on a map and work out how far the cattle may have travelled before arriving in London. Remember that they may have walked 300 kilometres or more, mostly through mountainous country, even before reaching Crieff or Falkirk. How are cattle transported today? Are there any cattle markets in your area? If so, try to visit one.

In November, surplus animals were slaughtered and their meat salted down for winter use.

A cattle sale in the Scottish Highlands. Cattle and sheep sales are interesting and lively occasions – and always worth visiting.

4 Dairy farming

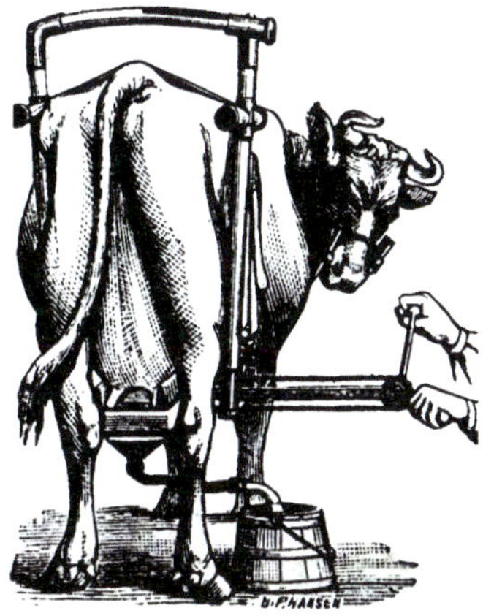

Above *A Danish milking machine of 1842. Do you think this was a better way of milking cows than by hand* **(below)** *? Which method do you think was more comfortable for the cow?*

Dairy cows are kept for their milk. In the past the dairy hand would sit on a three-legged stool, with his or her head tucked against the cow's side, and milk the cow into a bucket. Today, a dairy farmer simply stands and watches a machine milking eight or sixteen cows at once. Cows produce milk all the year round but mostly in spring, when the grass on which they feed is freshest, rich in nourishment and most plentiful. So in spring and early summer there is often a surplus of milk. What do you think happens to it?

Some is made into butter, cheese and yoghurt, and some of it is dried to make dried milk. Most farms used to make either butter or cheese or both. Butter was made by skimming the cream

off the milk, putting it into a churn and shaking or stirring it until it turned solid. Can you remember the old nursery rhyme which begins: 'Little Miss Muffet, Sat on a tuffet, Eating her curds and whey . . .' Curds are the material from which all cheeses are made. They are also quite easy to make.

Just stand a bottle of milk on the doorstep for a day or so in warm weather. It will 'go sour'. It turns, in fact, into curds and whey. The curds are the solid, jelly-like substance; the whey is the liquid that has become separated from them. Curds and whey are much the same as yoghurt. You can eat them, but you will need to add sugar, because of their sour taste. Or you can mash up the curds and let them stand a little longer, to form a kind of soft white cheese. Sprinkled with

Above *In a modern milking parlour, a farmer can milk many cows at the same time.*
Below *A butter churn from a farming catalogue of 1885. Use your local library to find pictures of old dairy equipment.*

sugar and eaten along with fresh strawberries, it tastes delicious.

Centuries ago, cattle were all-purpose animals. They were employed to pull ploughs and carts, they gave milk, and when they were killed their flesh was eaten. Today cattle have become specialized. Some belong to dairy breeds, which are bred to give lots of milk, and some belong to beef breeds, which are kept for their meat. Find out the names of as many of the dairy and beef breeds as you can. Make a note of how to distinguish the different breeds and try sketching them.

In the picture below, you can see four breeds of dairy cow. How many others can you find out about? Sketch each one and describe their main features. Do the same for breeds of beef cattle.

5 Sheep

A woman milking a sheep. It is rare for sheep to be kept for their milk these days. It was once a fairly common practice in Britain, and still is in many other countries.

Farmers today milk only cows and goats, as a rule, but in the past they also commonly milked sheep. In some countries they still do, and make cheese from the milk. Modern farmers keep sheep mainly for meat. Do you know what the meat of sheep is called? It is known as mutton (from the French word, *mouton*, meaning a sheep) or lamb, depending on the age of the animal.

What other purpose are sheep kept for? Are you wearing anything made of wool? Most sheep today have their wool clipped off by mechanical clippers. This is called shearing. The wool, shorn off in one piece, is called a fleece. Shearing usually takes place in late May or June, though later in hill regions. By then, the weather is growing warmer, and the sheep are glad to get rid of their heavy winter coats.

Shearing sheep with hand clippers at Denbigh in Wales, 1952. Notice that the sheep's legs are tied together to stop them struggling. Sheep shearing was done in much the same way for many hundreds of years.

Sheep shearing with mechanical clippers in the Cotswolds. The invention of mechnical clippers has meant that sheep can be shorn of their fleeces much quicker. The most skilful shearers can shear a sheep in about 4 minutes and around 150 sheep a day.

If the sheep are not shorn at the proper time they will gradually shed their wool by rubbing their bodies against walls, posts or trees, or having it torn off by brambles. In the past, women used to collect the wool from bushes and brambles or strip it from the sheep's back. They would then spin it to make woollen threads, which they would use for weaving or knitting into garments. Some women still do this.

A spinning wheel in use. Spinners used the wheel to turn wool into yarn. Weavers then took the yarn and wove it into cloth on their looms.

If you are able to visit an agricultural museum, you will probably see a spinning wheel. Perhaps someone will be there to demonstrate how it is used. There is another, simpler method of turning tufts of wool into thread. You need only two short rods, one of them split at the end. They are called spindle and distaff. The methods needs quite a lot of skill, though, and you will need an expert to show you how to do it.

If you live in a region where sheep are kept, you may be able to collect wool from fences, walls or thickets. Perhaps the whole class can arrange to do this. When you have the wool you may be able to get someone to show you how to card (comb it out) and perhaps to spin it as well. You could even experiment with dyeing the wool, using such things as old tea-bags, onion skins and herbs as dyes.

Below *A scene from a fifteenth-century stained glass window, showing weavers washing wool-cloth before dyeing it.*

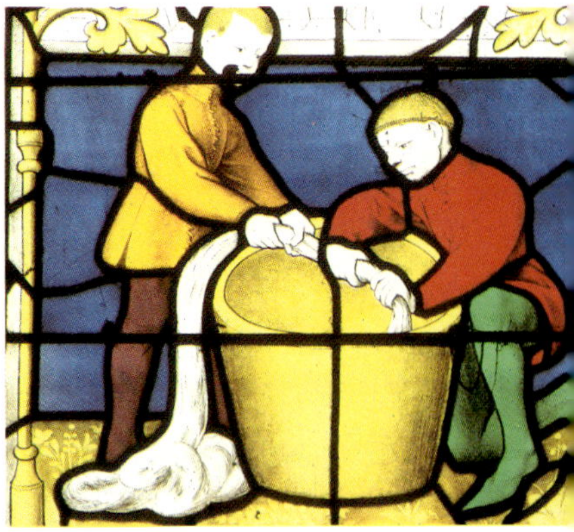

6 Crop farming

Above *A modern combine harvester cuts the crops and separates the grain from the stalks. In the past, these were two separate farming tasks, known as reaping and threshing.*

Grow some seeds in the school garden or in seed trays. If you can obtain the seed of a farm crop, such as wheat or barley, so much the better. Sow it in spring and watch it grow. You will notice that it first produces leaves; then a stem; then flowers (of a sort) at the tip of the stem. After a time the seeds which replace the flowers will ripen and grow hard. The plant withers and becomes brown. If you leave it alone, it will collapse and die. Then the seeds will fall into the soil and will produce new plants next year.

In the same way, farmers watch their crops as they grow. The farmer waits for the seed to ripen, and collects it before it falls to the ground. Collecting the seed is called harvesting it. When you talk with older people, ask them whether they have ever taken part in a harvest. Ask them what they remember about it. Did they enjoy harvesting? With their permission, you may use a tape recorder to record what they actually say.

Today, a combine-harvester trundles around a field, cutting the stalks and separating them from

Below *A harvest scene from a mediaeval calendar. The corn is cut, tied into sheaves and then hoisted onto the cart.*

the grain, a process which is called threshing. The combine-harvester gets its name from the fact that it combines both the cutting and the threshing of the grain. Your grandparents may remember when all the work had to be done by lots of people using hand-tools, rather than by one big machine.

A smaller machine, called a reaper or a binder pulled by horses, cut the stalks and tied them into sheaves. These had to be stood up in the fields in bundles, to dry for four or five days. They were then taken by horse-drawn wagons to the farmyard and built into ricks or stacks.

In winter the ricks were taken apart and the sheaves processed in a threshing machine, which beat the grain from the straw. Before threshing-machines were invented, the grain had to be

Above *A steam-powered threshing machine in operation near Canterbury, 1910.*

Below *This old mechanical reaper has been so well-preserved that it still works today.*

beaten out by a hand-tool, known as a flail. And before binders were invented, the standing crops were cut by a hand-tool known as a scythe.

The weather in late summer and autumn is often stormy and wet, so gathering the harvest was often a long struggle. Everybody was extremely glad when it was finished. They generally celebrated it with a feast. The harvest was the climax of the year and was marked by thanksgivings and festivities.

Do you know what use is made of the grain after harvesting? This depends on the type and quality of the grain: some is used for making bread, cakes, biscuits and breakfast cereals. Some is used for brewing beer or for distilling whisky. Much is fed to animals. Make a list of the grains grown in Britain and note what they are used for.

Above *A harvest song that was sung as the last wagon-load travelled homewards. When the last sheaf was picked up from the stubble, the Harvest Shout was raised:*
'Well ploughed!
Well sowed!
Well harrowed!
Well mowed!
And all carted safely into the barn with never a load throwed!
Hip-hiphip-hooray!'

7 Fertilizers

Fertilizers, which are now inserted into the soil by combine-drills, contain the basic plant-foods; namely, nitrate, potassium and phosphate. The plants need these in order to grow.

To test the effect they have, sow some grass seed in a tray of the poorest soil you can find (see figure 1). When the grass is about an inch high, add a sprinkling of nitrogen fertilizer to half the tray, leaving the other half untreated (2). You can obtain the fertilizer from a garden centre. Keep the tray well watered, and within a week or two you will see that the half which has had the benefit of nitrogen is taller and coloured a deeper green than the untreated half (3).

This experiment can be extended by sowing seeds in pots and varying the growing conditions as follows:	
(a) Pots to contain different soil types, ideally from sand to clay.	
(b) Pots containing the same soil type, such as loam, but varying the kind and amount of fertilizer added. One pot will have no fertilizer added.	
(c) Pots containing the same soil type but exposing them to different temperature conditions.	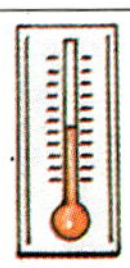
(d) Pots containing the same soil type but varying the amounts of water added.	
(e) Pots containing the same soil type but varying the exposure to light.	

Some simple activities with fertilizers which you can do at home or at school.

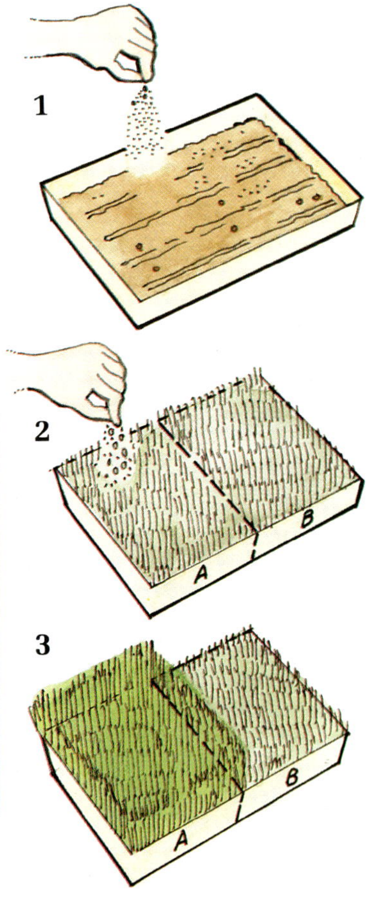

For centuries, animal manure was the only fertilizer used by farmers. If you keep a pet rabbit or guinea-pig, you can experiment with the manure from your pet's cage to see how it helps plants to grow.

Until about 150 years ago farmers had to manage without any knowledge of nitrate and other plant foods. What they had learned thousands of years earlier, however, was that animal manure helps plants to grow.

Have you ever kept a rabbit in a hutch? Perhaps you have rabbits at school. If so, repeat your grass-growing experiment. Select two adjoining plots in the school garden. When you dig them, bury in one of them a lot of soiled litter and droppings from the rabbit hutch. Add nothing to the other plot. Sow the grass seed, and when it grows you will see that the grass on the plot with the rabbit manure added is taller and greener than the other grass. The rabbit manure is supplying the grass with nitrogen.

Knowing this, farmers have for many centuries spread straw in the sheds and yards where their animals live. Then, from time to time, they carted the straw and dung, known as farmyard manure, to the fields and buried it in the soil by ploughing. Carting and spreading manure has always been – and still is – a major farm task.

Today, farmers use machines to spread manure over the fields before ploughing it into the soil.

The same benefits can be achieved by growing grass and allowing farm animals to graze it. The animals, of course, drop their dung where they graze. After a few years the soil has become greatly enriched, and the farmer then ploughs it and sows seeds of other crops in it.

Another excellent fertilizer is seaweed, which in some coastal areas (notably the West Highlands and Islands) is gathered from the seashore and ploughed into the soil.

In some coastal areas of Britain, farmers use seaweed as a fertilizer.

Above *A tractor with a special attachment for hedge-trimming. Modern farmers use machines to carry out a wide variety of tasks around the farm.*

8 Tools

Farmers now use huge and complicated machines to carry out many farming tasks. They have combine-harvesters, combine-drills, sprayers with long arms like aeroplane wings, multi-furrow ploughs, forage-harvesters like giant vacuum-cleaners, cultivators, rollers, potato-harvesters and other specialized equipment. There are even machines for harvesting apples, for trimming hedges and for digging post-holes. Compile a scrapbook on farm equipment and machinery. Farming magazines and journals are a good source of pictures.

Almost all the machines we have mentioned are quite modern inventions. From your local library or school library, borrow a book on farming

Below *Extracting the juice from apples with a transportable cider press at Pensford, Somerset, 1934. In the first part of the machine, the apples were broken up. Then the juice was squeezed from the resulting pulp in the second part.*

This mediaeval picture shows a man ploughing a field. The plough, pulled by a team of oxen, cuts a long deep trench into the soil known as a furrow.

100 or even 50 years ago. What tools or implements are the farm workers using?

Many of the new tools and machines have followed the invention of the internal combustion engine and the tractor. A hundred years ago, farm machinery (such as the threshing-machine) was operated by steam power, but most work was still done by hand or by animal power. Before that, work on farms had changed very little in thousands of years.

Below *Modern ploughs are attached to tractors and have several blades, so they can dig many furrows at the same time. How much faster do you think it is to plough this way than with a team of oxen, as in the picture above?*

Sowing seed by hand. The seed was carried in a container around the sower's neck and thrown in handfuls over the fields. This was known as broadcasting. Compare this picture with the one below.

Ask your grandparents or other elderly people whether they remember seeing these old-fashioned tools being used: hoes, spades, prongs, reap-hooks and pitchforks. Perhaps they themselves may have used them. If so, ask them to demonstrate how they were used. Of course, it is possible to buy modern versions of some of these tools in garden centres, but others you will find only in museums (see page 45). Try digging with a spade yourself, to see what it is like.

Below *On a modern farm, combine-drills like these are used to sow the seed in neat rows and deposit fertilizer alongside it, to help it grow.*

9 Weeds, pests, diseases

What is a weed? Farmers would probably tell you that a weed is a plant which grows where it is not wanted. A dandelion has a vivid golden flower, but no gardeners want dandelions on their lawn. Most weeds are wild plants. The farmer does not like them because they compete with the crops for food. Make a list of wild plants which you would call weeds. Make a collection of the most common ones and preserve them by pressing them between the pages of a heavy book.

Farmers like to keep their crops as clear of weeds as possible. Formerly they used to have to scrape out the weeds with a hoe. Now they employ big spraying machines. They spread (usually in liquid form) chemicals known as herbicides, which are designed to kill weeds.

Other chemicals spread by these spraying machines are pesticides and fungicides. Pesticides kill insects or bacteria. Fungicides kill the fungi which cause diseases.

Until the present century farmers had little protection for their crops. They had a rhyme which said they ought to sow four times as much seed

Opposite *An experiment to show the damage which can be done to crops by pests.*

Left *Although the Corn Marigold flowers in this wheat field may look attractive to us, they are still weeds as far as the farmer is concerned.*

Cabbage white experiment

In autumn, when the caterpillars of Cabbage White butterflies are plentiful, conduct the following experiment.

1 In a well-ventilated cage, place a recorded number caterpillars on cabbage leaves or nasturtium leaves. Weigh the leaves in advance. Try also to weigh the caterpillars (total weight, not individual).

2 Record the time it takes for the caterpillars to devour the leaves. Weigh the remains of the leaves and also the caterpillars. Compare these weights with your original figures. Does the increase in the caterpillars' weight equal that lost by the leaves?

3 If possible, supply the cabbage or nasturtium leaves from the school garden. Note the number of plants per square metre. How long would it take for your caterpillars to eat all the leaves on a patch of one square metre? Alternatively, as the caterpillars will probably be fully grown after two or three weeks of feeding, how many caterpillars would be needed to eat all the plants in a square metre in three weeks?

4 All pests tend to be very numerous and this experiment shows the damage that large numbers of small creatures can do. Farmers wage a constant war against these pests. If caterpillars are the farmer's enemies, then ichnuemon flies are the farmer's friends. The female ichnuemon fly lays her eggs in the chrysalid of a Cabbage White caterpillar. When the larvae hatch out they feed on the chrysalid. Many chrysalids are devoured in this way. This is known as biological pest control.

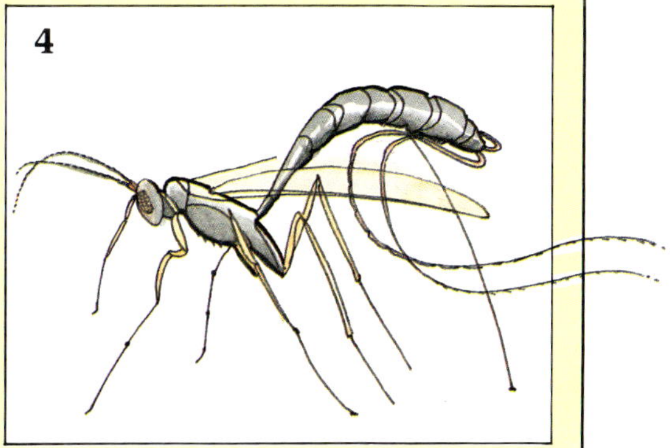

as was really needed (can you think why this was necessary?):

'One for the pigeon; one for the crow;
One to rot; and one to grow.'

Many people think that farming has now gone to the other extreme, for they say that the chemicals also kill off many interesting creatures and plants. But few farmers would like to return entirely to the old days. In the war against weeds, for instance, many farm hands used to have to work hard all the summer, chopping away at weeds with hoes. It would be very expensive for modern farmers to do this because wages are so much higher today.

Farm animals, too, used to suffer from many ailments which are now prevented by injections, just as you are vaccinated against such ailments as whooping-cough. Below are a few remedies which were used to treat diseases affecting live-stock. Can you find any more in your local library?

Above *Until the invention of herbicides, weeds had to be removed using just a few simple tools, as you can see in this picture.*

Below *Some old remedies for sick animals. There were others for human ailments, too: 'Back ache – rub back with the liquor obtained by pickling snails'. Can you find any others?*

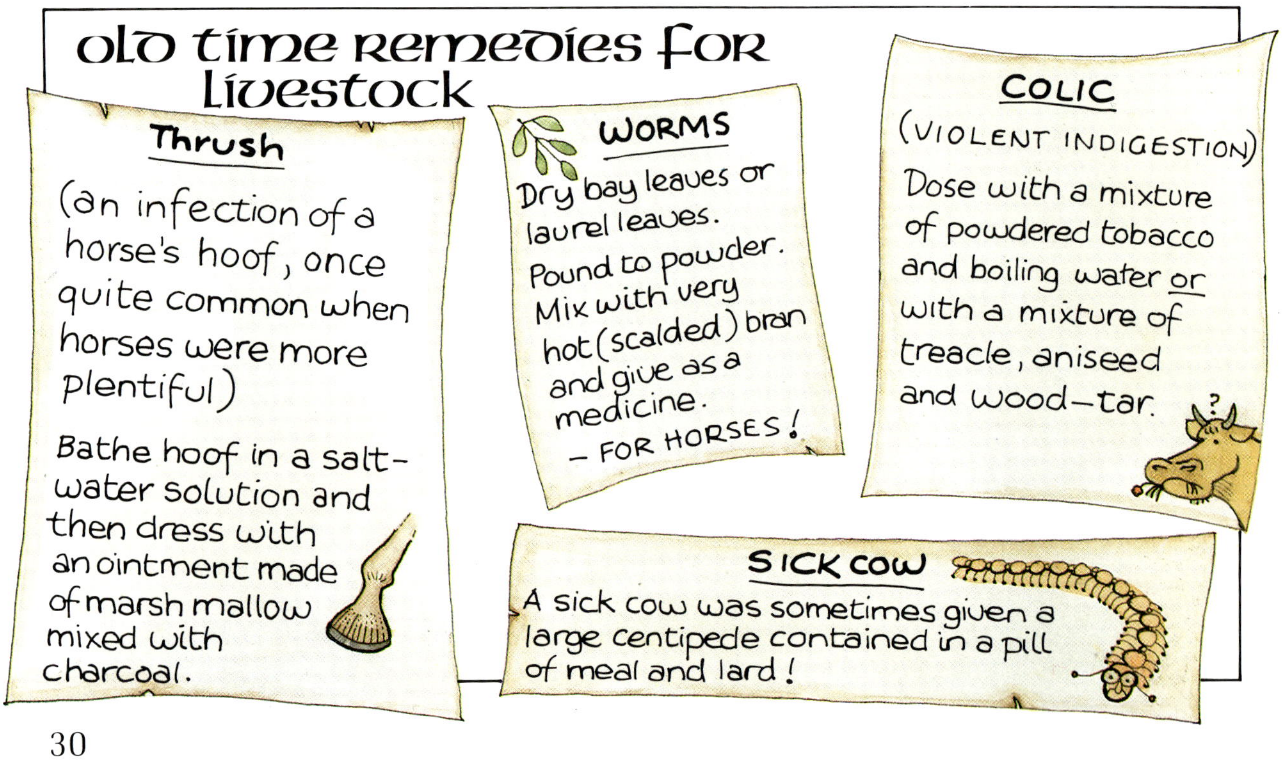

10 Farm buildings

In the past, and in some instances even in this present century, farm animals and people had to live together under one roof. In the Scottish Highlands, for instance, crofters' houses were divided into the living quarters of the crofter's family and stabling for the animals. Sometimes the family was only separated from the animals by a low partition. In some English counties people and animals were housed on different floors. The family and farm workers slept in lofts over the cattle-sheds and stables – very warm in winter!

Today, farmers need buildings for many different purposes. These will vary according to the type of farm, but may include:

- shelter for cattle and horses in winter.
- places where fattening animals, such as pigs, can be fed and where poultry can find shelter and be fed in winter.
- storage for sacks of grain, bales of hay and other foods.
- milking sheds for dairy cows.

A 'black house' on the Isle of Lewis, in the Hebrides. These houses had low stone walls with roofs of turf or thatched heather. The families who lived in them were poor and shared their houses with their animals. One end of the house was for the family, the other for the animals.

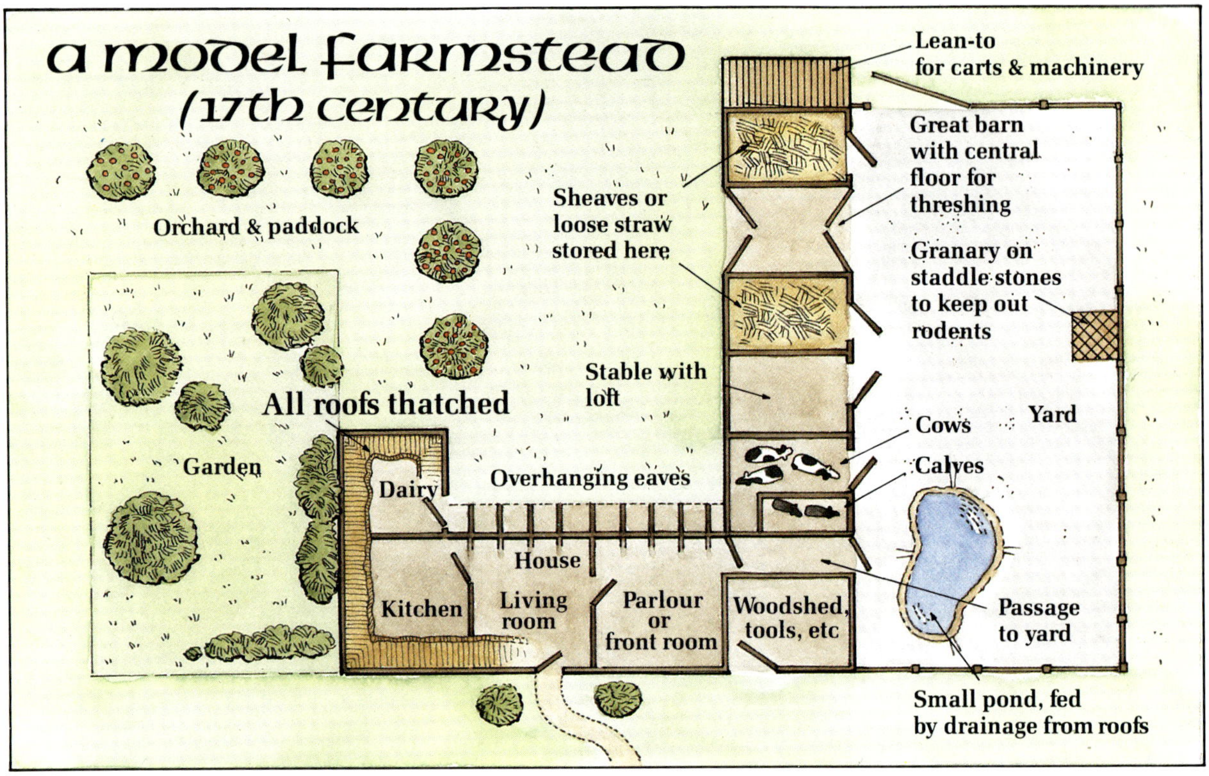

- shelter for farm implements and equipment.
- specialized workshops; for example, where cheese can be made or machinery repaired.

There have been many changes in farm buildings over the years. Some specialized buildings, such as oast-houses and malt-houses, have become more or less obsolete. Grain silos have tended to replace barns for storage. Now buildings have had to be designed or old ones adapted for storing silage, while the sheds for housing big farm machinery need to be much larger than was formerly necessary.

At some point during your studies, it will be very helpful for you to visit a farm. When you do, prepare for it by making a list of the things you expect to see. In particular, study the layouts of farms and see how everything you have learned about farms fits in. It will be useful to have a plan

Above *The layout of a typical farmstead in the seventeenth century. What differences do you think you would notice if you compared this with the plan of a modern farm?*

Right *Some examples of old farm buildings. What others have you seen? Try to sketch them and make a note of where you saw them.*

OLD FARM BUILDINGS

1. Scottish Crofter's house

2. Malt house

3. Oast house

4. Seventeenth-century farmhouse

5. Old thatched barn

6. Staddle-stone barn

7. Tithe barn

of the farm you are going to visit. How are the fields arranged in relation to the farm buildings? Are all the buildings modern or are there some old ones still standing? Make a sketch of the farm, paying particular attention to any unusual old farm buildings you may come across.

Where do the different kinds of animals live? Consider, for instance, how the cows are moved from the fields to the collecting yard, and then into the milking parlour and out again? Where does the drainage go?

You must ask the farmer to give you the basic facts about the farm, such as, for instance, how many hectares of land there are, how many cows, sheep, pigs or poultry are kept, and how many hectares are used for each type of crop. The farmer may also know how the farm has changed in the recent past. If one family has occupied the land for several generations, you may even be able to find out what the farm was like at the beginning of this century. Back at school use your imagination to draw a picture of how the farm looked in the past. Compare this with your sketch of the farm as it is today. Is it well designed, or do you think you can suggest any improvements?

Below, you can see aerial photographs of two different types of farms. What type of farming do you think is carried out on each farm? What differences/similarities do you notice in the layouts of the two farms?

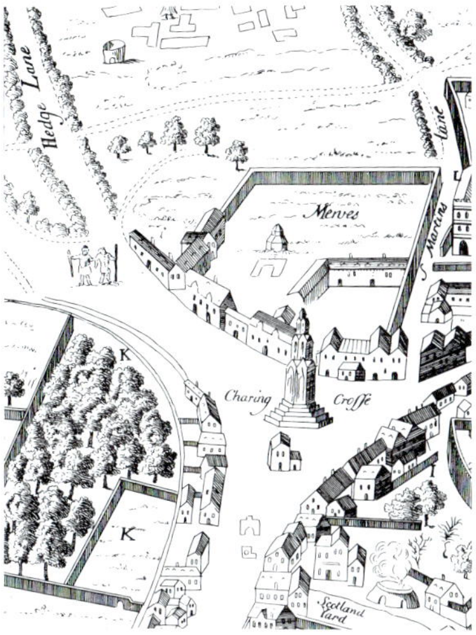

Above *Old maps may show that your part of town was once fields and trees. This map shows just how few buildings there were in the Charing Cross area of London in Elizabethan times.*
Below *Smithfields cattle market in 1855.*

11 In the town

Farmers now sell their produce to organizations such as the Milk Marketing Board or to wholesale merchants. In former times they took it to the nearest town to sell. In most towns there was a market place, usually in the middle of the town, where they displayed their goods. Is there one in your town?

Perhaps the market place has now disappeared, but the sections of the town used for the purpose may have retained their old names. Make a list of any you can find. There may be a Sheep Street; a Butcher Row; a Poultry Cross; a Shambles (an old word for a slaughterhouse); a Corn Exchange; a Cheese Market. Look out also for Market Street, Market Place, Marketgate and Cowgate. Here, the word 'gate' does not mean that there was really an opening or a gate. It was actually a misspelling

Above *The sixteenth-century yarn market at Dunster in Somerset.*

Left *Chichester Market Cross was built in 1501. Many towns still have buildings like these to remind us of their past connections with farming and its products.*

Below *Street names are often good clues to the history of your area.*

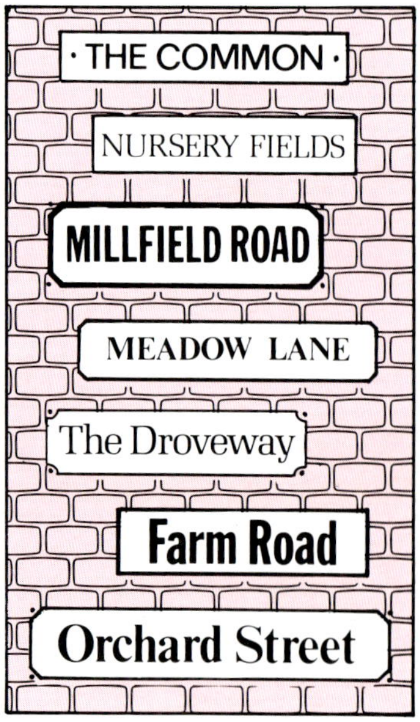

of the word 'gait', a name applied to the way leading to a market, along which cattle and sheep were driven. There may even be a Market Inn, too.

Ask an elderly person if they have any memories of such names, or even of the places being used for markets. And at your local library enquire about old town maps, showing the names of streets and markets, many years ago.

12 Festivals & traditions

In many parts of the country old festivals and traditions are still celebrated today. You can often see Morris dancers performing in the summer months. Their stamping dance was supposed to wake up the good spirits of the soil so that they would produce a plentiful harvest.

In the old-time farming calendar, the year started with Plough Monday (the first Monday after Twelfth Night), when the ploughs started work after Christmas. Candlemas Day (2 February) was the traditional date for the start of the lambing season.

In mediaeval times, Lent was a season of fasting. This was for practical as well as religious reasons, because food became scarce by the end of March. March has always been the sowing month. In April cows and sheep were turned out to feed on the new spring grass.

Before silage was made, May (which is now the chief silage-making month) was fairly free from farm work, so it was a time for many country festivals and sports. Some examples are May Day, Morris dancing, Rogationtide and Whitsuntide. Look up books to see what people did on each of these occasions.

June and early July was the main haymaking period. Towards the end of July the harvest began.

August was the main harvest month, though harvesting continued into September, when ploughing began again. Michaelmas (29 September) was the traditional end of the farming year, when farms changed hands and when farm workers changed jobs. There were harvest-home feasts and harvest festivals. It was also the season of fairs, when surplus sheep and cattle were sold.

Ploughing continued into October, when winter wheat was sown. November was the slaughter month, when surplus animals were killed and salted down for winter food. Hedges were trimmed and the farm tidied up. Bonfire Night, on 5 November, gave a chance to burn up the rubbish. December was a busy month when fat stock were prepared for the Christmas markets.

These dates are true for southern and central England but further north and in mountain districts the farming activities would be a month or more later. The dates of some of the festivals were different, too. Make an illustrated farming calendar relating to your own area. Include the main tasks and festivals that occurred each month.

Below *May Day celebrations at Lynn in Norfolk, 1827.*

Rhymes and sayings

'In the barn on Candlemas day, should be half the straw and half the hay'

(By Candlemas Day, 2 Feb, winter is only half over)

'When the cuckoo sings on an empty bough, Keep your hay, and sell your cow.'

(A sign of late spring, when animal fodder is scarce)

'who sows in May Gets little that way'

(May is too late for sowing most crops)

'ICE IN NOVEMBER TO BEAR A DUCK, NOTHING AFTER BUT SLUSH AND MUCK.'

'Copper under heather, Silver under gorse, Gold under bracken.'

(Meaning that the natural vegetation is a good indication of the fertility of the soil. Generally fairly accurate.)

13 A mediaeval village

The remains of a mediaeval village and field system near Dartmoor's Hound Tor, in Devon. Such remains are often shown on Ordnance Survey maps by the words 'field system'.

In the Middle Ages the farmland around most villages was divided into three big fields. One was devoted to growing wheat; another to growing barley or oats; and the third was 'fallow', which means that it grew no crops at all. Next year the cropping plan for the fields was switched around. The idea of the fallow field was that by allowing the soil to rest for a year it replenished its fertility. During the fallow year it grew grass and weeds, on which the village animals grazed.

This was the system for most of England. In mountain districts and in Scotland and Wales it was rather different. There, little wheat was

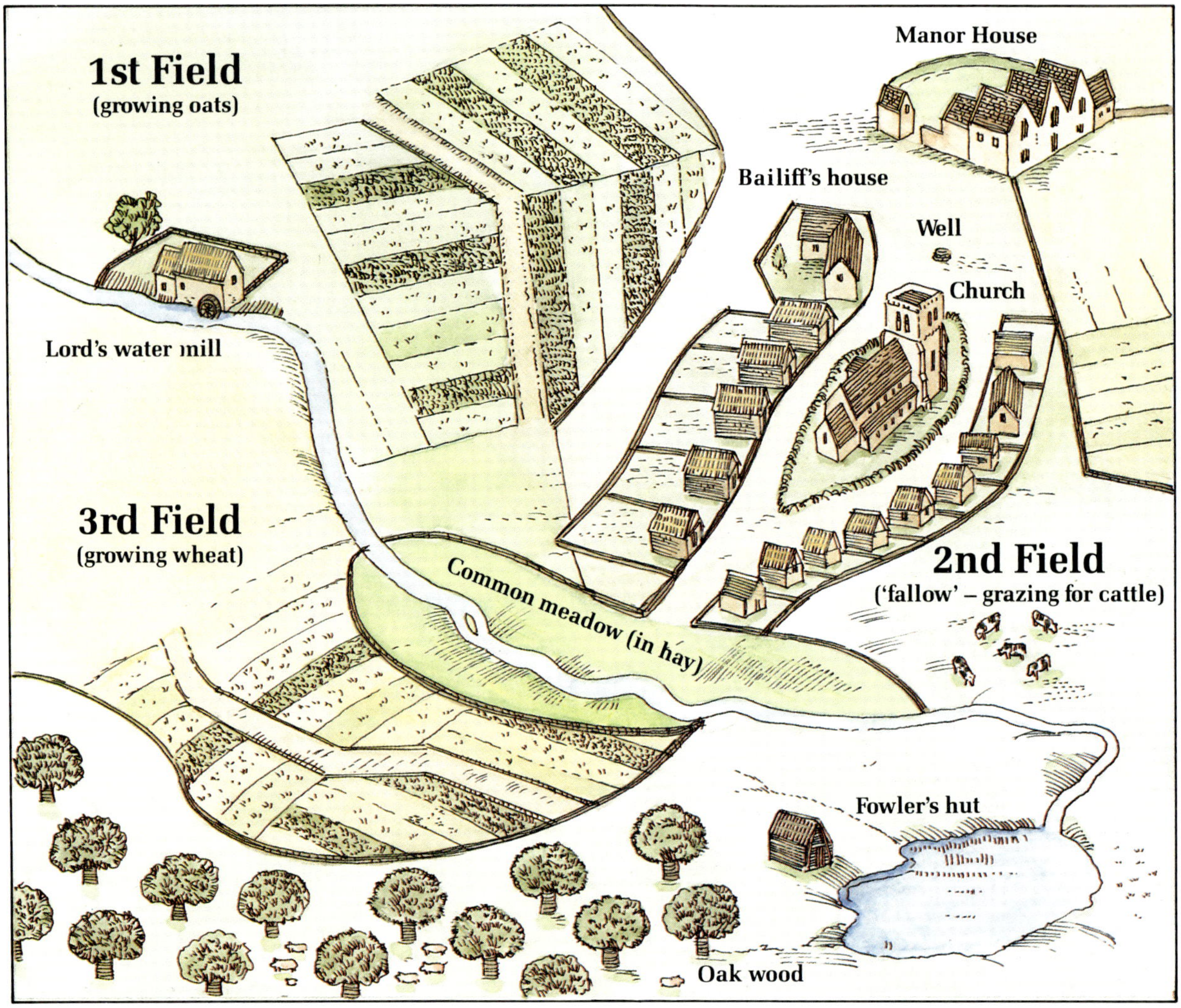

grown, and the land was divided into only two big fields. In many instances there was no fallow land. The best crops were grown in the field nearest the village, which was manured with all the kitchen rubbish and animal dung.

Draw a sketch of a mediaeval village, with three big fields around it. Now think of the villagers who would do the work and grow the crops. Suppose there were twenty of them. How would you arrange things so that each had a fair share?

In fact, the villagers arranged matters by dividing each of the big fields into a series of smaller plots, usually shaped as long strips, which were

How the land around an English mediaeval village might have been used under the three field system. The Manor House was the home of the lord of the manor. The bailiff looked after the lord's estate, while the fowler earned his living catching wild birds.

easier to plough. Each of the villagers was allotted several strips in each field, so that every year he or she would have so many plots growing wheat, so many growing barley and so many bearing no crop at all.

On your plan, divide each of the big fields into a number of smaller strip-shaped ones. One of the farmers is named Adam Green, so mark his initials on a certain number of strips. Four in each field. But wait. It would never do for Adam Green to have his four plots in the best soil of each field, leaving his neighbour, Bill Black, with four on the poorer soils. So the rule was that no farmer should have adjoining plots. The plots had to be scattered about the fields, as far away from each other as possible. Each village had an area of common land, on which the villagers were allowed to keep an agreed number of grazing animals, such as cattle, sheep, geese and – in woodlands – pigs. Where fields were fallowed, the fallow field was regarded as common land for the following year.

When we go out into the countryside you can often see traces of the old strips still visible in the fields. You will also find traces of them marked on old maps. If you are able to visit a farm, look for traces of farming practices a long ago.

A mediaeval cooking scene. Only the rich could afford to eat much meat, often cooked with lots of spices and herbs. Poorer people had a much plainer diet of coarse bread, cheese, oatmeal, soups and ale.

Pigs foraging for acorns in an oakwood. The villagers' woodland was often used as a common area where pigs could roam freely in search of food.

14 Conclusion

In exploring the farming past of Britain it will be helpful to understand the broad divisions into which the agricultural developments of the past can be placed.

1 In Neolithic times (4000–1800 BC) people began to grow crops and gradually changed from being hunters to farmers.

2 Improvements occurred gradually over several thousands of years, reaching a fairly high peak of development in Roman times. Farming methods and practices were much the same in the time of Queen Elizabeth I (1558–1603) as they were in Roman times. The chief differences were in the system of land tenure and field arrangement.

3 In Stuart times (1603–1714) new field crops,

Eighteenth-century sheep and cattle were much smaller than modern breeds. Robert Bakewell (left) introduced 'selective breeding': only the best bulls and rams were allowed to mate with females of their species. The weight and quality of cattle and sheep improved steadily with these methods (see phase 5).

such as clover and turnips, were introduced.

4 During the eighteenth and early nineteenth centuries the old system of land tenure and field arrangement (see page 39) was completely changed. Fields were enclosed and grouped to form farms such as we see today. This happened through a series of Enclosure Acts of Parliament.

5 The new arrangements triggered off many far-reaching changes which became known as the Agricultural Revolution. Scientific breeding of livestock resulted in vastly improved breeds of cattle, sheep, pigs, poultry and horses. Similar principles applied to plant-breeding resulted in crops capable of producing much greater yields.

6 The use of steam power, which started the Industrial Revolution, had, at first, little direct application on farms. However, a little later, in the mid-nineteenth century, threshing engines were introduced to do a job which had previously been done by men. And when railways were established, the milk train brought milk from distant places and did away with the necessity of having dairy farms in or very near towns. Railways also made it much easier to transport agricultural produce.

An American ship unloads its cargo of wheat into a grain elevator on the River Thames, 1880. Such shipments had important effects on farming in Britain (see phase 7, overleaf).

7 A great depression in agriculture began around 1875, when shipments of wheat from America and Canada and of refrigerated meat from Australia, New Zealand and Argentina began to arrive in Britain. Dependence on British farms thus ended and much land fell out of cultivation.
8 With the exception of the period of the First World War (1914–18), this depression lasted until the beginning of the Second World War (1939). Then it became necessary to grow as much food as possible in Britain, to avoid having to import it from overseas. Can you think why it would have been difficult to import food from overseas during wartime?
9 Since 1945, the end of the Second World War, there have been many changes to farming methods with the introduction of massive new machines, improved plants, new crops, better livestock and a wide range of chemicals for the control of weeds, pests and diseases.

A green woodpecker feeding its young. Setting aside parts of the countryside as nature reserves and conservation areas provides safe places for plants, animals and birds to live and breed. It is a valuable way of using land that is not required to produce food.

In your explorations you will have found that many older people remember quite well what farming was like before phase 9 of our time chart. For information about the earlier periods you will have had to rely on books, old maps, visits to agricultural museums and on noting the traces of farming in the past in the countryside around you.

Today another agricultural revolution is taking place. Food and other agricultural produce are being imported from many other countries, and big farm surpluses are building up. There is no longer need for British farms to produce enough food to feed the entire population, and farmers fear a return to the depressions noted in phases 7 and 8. New uses for land are being urgently sought, two of the most commonly suggested being nature conservation and forestry.

Above *Rare breed farms try to preserve traditional breeds of animals which might otherwise die out.*
Below *Goats being displayed at an agricultural show. Visiting one of these shows is perhaps one of the best ways of finding out about the many different types of farming there are.*

Places to visit

1 Local libraries, where you can consult books and local maps.
2 Local museums. Many of these now have agricultural sections or displays, particularly showing scenes of old-time villagers at work or at home.
3 Farms. During the summer many farms organize open days. Visitors are welcome and are sometimes taken around the farm on trailers. You can often watch cows being milked and calves and being fed. Watch your local paper for advertisements. It may be possible to arrange farm trips through the local branch of the National Farmers Union.
4 Town farms. Some towns and boroughs have farm designed to attract and educate children.
5 Heavy horse centres. These are like farms, but exist primarily to show off heavy horses and their equipment.
6 Rare breed farms. These specialize in keeping traditional breeds of livestock, some of which would otherwise be in danger of dying out.
7 Agricultural Shows. These range from national and international shows to local ones. They are mostly held in summer and autumn. Farmers compete with each other to show the best cattle and other livestock, and there are numerous trade stalls exhibiting the latest machinery.

Further reading

Bolwell, Laurie & Lines, Clifford, *The Countryside in the Past* (Wayland, 1987)
Boyden, Peter B., *The Children's Book of Domesday England* (Kingfisher, 1985)
Butcher, T. K., *Country Life* (Batsford, 1970)
Pluckrose, Henry, *Seen in Britain* (Mills & Boon, 1977)
Sauvain, Philip, *Looking Around in Town and Country* (Watts, 1975)
Whitlock, Ralph, *A Calendar of Country Customs* (Batsford, 1978)
Whitlock, Ralph, *The English Farm* (Dent, 1984)
Whitlock, Ralph, *Farming in History* (Wayland, 1984)

Glossary

Ancestor A person far back in one's family history.
Arable Land that is ploughed.
Bacteria Tiny organisms, some of them harmful, which are present everywhere.
Binder A machine for cutting standing crops and tying them into sheaves.
Bronze Age The term used to describe the time when weapons and tools were made of bronze. In Britain it lasted from about 2000 to 500 BC.
Combine-drill A machine for sowing seed and fertilizer together.
Combine-harvester A machine for cutting and threshing crops in one operation.
Common Land Uncultivated land belonging to a community, where members of the community have rights to pasture grazing animals.
Curds and whey Substances formed by the action of acids or heat on milk.
Distaff A cleft stick for holding wool or flax when spinning by hand.
Domesticate To tame.
Drovers A person hired to drive cattle or sheep to and from market.
Fallow Land left uncropped for a period, in order to give the soil a rest.
Flail A hand-operated implement for threshing grain.
Fleece The woolly coat of a sheep.
Forage-harvester A machine which gathers up fresh grass which has been cut for making silage.
Fungicide A chemical for killing fungi, especially those responsible for diseases.
Herbicide A chemical for killing weeds.
Horticulture (also known as market gardening) The growing or culture of vegetables, fruit and flowers.
Industrial Revolution The change in Britain which came about in the eighteenth and nineteenth centuries, when the country became a manufacturing nation instead of a farming nation.
Land tenure The possession of land and the terms and conditions under which it is held.

Lent A Christian festival, lasting for forty weekdays before Easter, which was traditionally a time of fasting.

Loam A fertile soil containing some vegetable matter.

Malt-house A building for preparing and storing malt produced from barley, for use in brewing beer or ale.

May Day A celebration marking the beginning of spring, held in the first week of May.

Mediaeval Of, or having to do with the Middle Ages (approximately AD 1000–1500)

Michaelmas The feast of St Michael (29 September); the beginning of autumn and an important quarter day, when farms changed hands and farm workers changed their jobs.

Morris dancing Traditional country dancing.

Neolithic Belonging to the New Stone Age, approximately 4000–1800 BC.

Nitrate One of the essential plant foods.

Oast-house A building containing a kiln for drying hops, in preparation for making beer.

Obsolete A thing is obsolete if it has gone out of use.

Pesticide A chemical for killing insect pests.

Phosphate Another essential plant food.

Plough Monday A traditional festival, when ploughs started work again after the Christmas holiday.

Potassium The third of the three essential plant foods.

Rogationtide A spring-time religious festival, when a priest led people in procession around a village, blessing the growing crops.

Shearing Cutting the wool off sheep.

Sheaves Cut corn tied together in small bundles.

Silage Green grass preserved in a pit or clamp by compressing it.

Silos Tower-like buildings used for storing grain.

Spindle A straight stick for winding thread when spinning by hand.

Staddle stones A conical stone, with a flat, circular stone on top. Staddle stones supported barns, granaries and hay stacks about 0.5m above the ground to protect them from vermin and damp ground conditions.

Subsistence farming Farming mainly for one's own needs, without attempting to produce a surplus for sale.

Wholesale merchants People who buy goods in large quantities and then sell them in smaller quantities to other traders.

Index

Picture Acknowledgements
The publishers would like to thank the following for supplying pictures: Aerofilms 34 (left and right); Aldus Archive 10 (British Museum), 16 (bottom, British Museum), 20 (top), 26 (top, British Museum), 41 (bottom, British Museum); Bodleian Library 12 (top); Bruce Coleman 7 (Jane Burton), 17 (Mark Boulton), 19 (top, Mark Boulton), 20 (bottom, Inigo Everson); Mary Evans 21, 25 (bottom), 35 (bottom); Farmers Weekly 11 (bottom); GeoScience Features (right), 18 (top), 29; Hutchison Picture Library 12 (bottom), 31, 37; The Mansell Collection 41 (top); Oxford Scientific Films 9 (top), 23 (top), 44; Ann Ronan 38 (bottom), 43; Ronald Sheridan 18 (bottom), 36 (top left); TOPHAM *cover*, 5 (left), 6, 11 (top), 14 (top), 23, 24, 45 (top and bottom); University of Reading, Institute of Agricultural History and Museum of Rural Life 44; Tim Woodcock 36 (top right), 39; Zefa 4, 9 (bottom). All artwork is by Stephen Wheele, except 15 (Anna Jupp), 26 (bottom, Anne Howard) and 27 (bottom, Anne Howard). The remaining pictures are from the Wayland Picture Library.